Stay a little longer

Written by Zoe Cawley

Dedication

*In memory of all those who have lost their battle
With their mental Health,
Friends Who I've lost and in honour of my friends and
everyone
Else in this world who chooses to stay
And fights their head every single day.
Thank-you.*

Message from the author...

Dear the people reading,
to those who suffer with their mental health,
To those that love or care for someone who suffers,
I hope this brings you some kind of comfort and positivity
And to feel understood by someone,
I hope these poems make you feel less alone.
It's okay to ask for help
and to accept it, you're worthy
and deserving of it and so much more,
You are cared for, you are loved
And there will be someone to listen to you.
So keep fighting
And stay a little longer.

Love Zoe x

Children in older skin

I know at times I may be a difficult person to love,
but trust me when I love,
I love with all my heart, I am more than just these broken parts,
Or just damaged goods.
I'm just a lost soul trying desperately to be understood,
Because we are all just children in older skin,
And some of us are trying to heal that child from within,
Because I may be a pain, and I say the same things over and over again,
Asking for reassurance,
Just wanting to be loved and accepted the way I wasn't back then,
By Self-sabotaging or self-destructing
I thought it would make it easier to breathe,
I always expect people to just leave,
Growing up in a chaotic environment made no room for peace,
Growing up with inadequate care makes your self-worth decrease,
Although I may have a tough exterior,
I don't think of myself as being anywhere near superior,
Some of us are just trying to grieve
for the love and care that we didn't receive,
The walls I've built are just protection from rejection,
From the abandonment and loss, I fear I'm
going to get,
It isn't as easy as pushing a button on hurt or childhood trauma
and pressing reset,
And there may be things that some adults know,
But some things we haven't learnt yet,
That we are allowed to cry even if we don't know why
and there's no such thing as being too sensitive,
That they don't hate us because of an unanswered text or call,
That we aren't unloveable, and someone will be there to catch us if we fall.
So I know I may be a hard person to understand and love
But all there is a little Kid inside,
Who's always felt the need to hide behind a disguise,
She felt that she was too broken to be loved,
Far too broken to heal That is the way she sometimes still feels,
But maybe I don't need to be fixed,
I just maybe need to be loved and cared for
the way that I should have been,
To finally feel seen,
Although I don't believe I deserve love and care
Because I may feel too broken and that People won't be there
Although I may be hard to love and
I feel like I'm shattered into broken parts,

When I love, I love with all my heart,
We are all just children in older skin,
And some of us are just trying to heal that child from within.

Getting better

A thing I've found hard to explain was my fear of getting better,
It's not like I wanted to necessarily be this way,
it's just I can't remember or imagine ever being okay.
As human beings, we hate the unknown,
And when you have endured pain and trauma for a long time
We take the pain and the chaos
And eventually, it feels like home,
As painful as it may be, I almost became attached to the misery,
Without sadness and pain, who am I?
and I was scared to find out,
Leaving me with lots of doubt.
Change can be a scary thing,
What will changing bring?
Sometimes it's accepting for a while that change can sting.
Letting go of behaviours and thought patterns
that felt so familiar to you.
Letting go of coping mechanisms that helped you get through,
You can feel lost for a little while, but one day you will again smile,
I guess it's weighing it up,
We could stay the same,
Being in pain brings
Familiarity and safety and control,
Or we let go, we don't know for a little bit
and we see if maybe letting go does provide us with something more,
Something worth fighting for,
It's okay to be scared of getting better.
I thought that thought made me crazy for a long time
But being happy isn't a crime.
It's just not something you are used to feeling
It's okay to feel scared, numb, anxious,
terrified, excited, happy it all comes with healing,
The unknown can eventually become Known
and just know you're not alone
And pain and chaos doesn't have to be your forever home.

Love you don't have to earn

Something I'm having to learn,
Is that love I don't have to earn,
That people loving me or caring about me isn't based on kilograms,
That the right people will just love me for the way that I am,
That worry and care doesn't have the same definition and meaning,
We can get attached to our mental illness,
Especially when it's been probably the only consistent thing in our lives,
We were meant to get consistency and care in a different form
But now we mix worry with care and think that is the norm,
You get to the point where you think if you weren't mentally Ill
then you won't be loved or looked after anymore,
And that's due to the fact of not being loved properly before,
It's okay to be okay, it doesn't mean people will go away,
People will stay,
you getting better and them not worrying as much
just simply means that they are not scared of losing you
to this illness every minute of every day.
There will still be people there and they will still care.
You are loved and cared for, for you
Not just for the things you are going through,
When we didn't get loved the way that we should
It makes us wonder if anyone ever would,
Or even if they could,
You do not need to be falling apart in order to be loved,
You will meet people who love you
and they don't always have to be blood.
Love doesn't need to be earned
Everyone else gets loved and cared for
and not only because they are Ill and/or people are concerned,
And it is a hard lesson but it needs to be learned,
That you will find people who love you and care,
Not because of your diagnosis or symptoms,
people will still be there,
To learn that love you don't have to earn,
That worry and care are not the same
You will still be loved even if you're not in pain.

Empty pill bottles.

What people need to try and understand is
depression isn't always empty pill bottles And goodbye letters,
Depression isn't just crying all day,
sometimes it's masking and pretending you're okay.
Depression isn't just being sad,
Depression can be having a smile,
To try and cover up the pain they've been enduring for a while,
It can be being the class clown,
To try and turn other people's frowns upside down,
It can be isolating from family and friends
It can be feeling like they want things to end,
Not brushing their hair for days,
Also can be pushing loved ones away,
Taking everything to heart
They feel like their life is falling apart,
Sometimes too sad to move,
you can't see it, But their pain they shouldn't have to prove.
It can look like they are productive
and like to keep busy all the time
but that's a way of dealing with their mind,
A distraction based on fear,
Fear of the thoughts in their brain.
If they stop they'll have to deal with their pain.
They say it's the happy ones you have to look out for,
Which couldn't be any more true.
They are in so much pain and no one even knew.
Depression is a silent killer,
Because the 'sad ones' are 'iller'.
What do we do?
wait till it's too late to make a change.
Because to you someone who has so much energy who makes jokes,
Who paints a smile but also has depression you find strange.
all you have to do is be kind
because you don't know what's going on in someone's mind.

Be kind

Some people in life aren't always that kind,
but what you'll find is
Like Dr Seuss said,
Those that mind don't matter and those that matter don't mind
And in life,
you get to the stage where a chapter has finished
and you're ready to turn the page,
And when you start putting yourself first or starting to set boundaries
You may lose people you care about,
Which may leave you with doubt.
Doubting whether you are doing the right thing,
Scared and unsure of what putting yourself first will bring,
But just because you don't know,
That doesn't mean you shouldn't allow yourself to grow
And sometimes we get used to the chaos,
which is why it's so hard to let our experiences go
but it's about time you start allowing yourself to heal,
to feel how you feel,
But those that matter
love and encourage that you that has got through
and in that journey of healing if you lose people along the way
that is okay as dr Seuss would say,
Those that mind don't matter and those that matter don't mind
Be kind, to others of course but mostly to yourself
because you deserve that just like everyone else

Validation

Your validation isn't based on whether you've been restrained,
by mental health professionals that are trained,
Your validation isn't based on having a hospital admission
or how severe were the mental health conditions,
Your validation isn't based on how long you have suffered for,
Your validation isn't based on someone suffering more.
Your validation isn't based on how many actions
or behaviours you've acted upon.
Your validation isn't based on how long.
How long you have been suffering,
You are valid because you have suffered.
You haven't ended up in a hospital?
Okay, but you're still struggling.
Still fighting to win.
Don't stay in bed all day? But you have depression,
Okay but your still struggling and lots of people do that,
and anyone who says people who have depression
are all bed ridden needs a lesson.
You have an eating disorder but you've eaten,
it doesn't mean you are okay
or the thoughts have magically just gone away,
Something that makes you smile for a second
doesn't mean you're hurting less.
You're just trying to do your best.
Your suicidal but your still breathing,
your still valid and I thank you for not leaving.
Valid even if your pain some people don't see.
Valid even if some people don't believe,
Valid because you've suffered,
Valid because only you know your truth,
And you don't need to give people any proof,
Getting on with your life or trying to thrive rather than survive
does not mean what happened didn't happen,
Doesn't make you less valid or impact your validation.
People will see you've got through.
And it wasn't easy but a difficult thing to do.
You're valid okay? You know the truth, no one can take that away.
You're valid no matter what and that's all I've got to say.

Nothing is forever

not everything in life is forever,
The friendship group you made in high school
may not stay together,
Life can be up and down and change just like the weather,
Unfortunately sometimes good things don't last
that's the same with the pain you've experienced in the past,
That passes too,
They say life is a roller coaster and it's true
We are all just trying our hardest to push through,
But when we've learnt that,
we can surrender and say okay and ride the wave
and whatever may come your way,
And just because what you knew as the good
has come to an end
it doesn't mean there isn't any more happiness
or good to come just around the bend,
Just some things in life don't turn out the way
we expected them to
and change can be scary and new.
but just because things could have been different
doesn't mean they would have been better
or would have been much more great
which I know you have probably spent hours having that debate,
Just because life didn't turn out the way you expected it to,
Doesn't mean there can't be something new,
Doesn't mean the new and what's to come isn't exciting,
It's okay to let the light in,
Put your hand in the air while your on this rollercoaster
even if it gives you a scare,
Expect highs but also lows
And remember just because the good maybe done,
hang on tight because new good is to come.

Trauma makes us traumatised

Why is the narrative that trauma makes us strong,
In my opinion that's wrong,
trauma makes us traumatised.
The strength part comes from within,
From the individual,
And that isn't learnt from a manual or a module.
The strength it took us to push through
Enduring pain and no one even knew
They say 'well everything happens for a reason'
That it'll all get better with the changes of the seasons,
But the trauma I've experienced will be with me forever
even with the changes in the weather,
Trauma doesn't make us invincible, it makes us vulnerable.
And no one can take your trauma away from you at all
Because if your trauma traumatised you
then it doesn't matter if to others it seems insignificant or small,
We aren't strong because of our trauma,
We did that.
With the thoughts the pain and the memories we sat,
Our trauma can make us depressed
or make us become this performer
We can use humour to Cope,
If we indulge in that comfort of sadness.
We have to be careful because it can become a slippery slope,
It can make us scared, alone,
not knowing how to deal with our emotions
because we were never shown.
There's no timeframe to deal with trauma,
So if you think trauma makes us strong,
Your wrong,
Trauma makes us traumatised.

Beauty standards

I never saw myself as someone who was beautiful,
I was never the girl who was cool in school.
I don't have a perfect belly, or I'm not like the girls you see on telly.
I don't have perfect skin,
but people say it's not about what you look like on the outside
but who you are within,
I wouldn't say I have a lot or any beauty,
But this is me,
The not so perfect, not fitting beauty standards me.
I'm not a piece of art but I try to have a good heart.
Trying to be perfect or look slightly okay.
Trying to make myself a certain way.
Trying to lose weight, have great hair,
Reaching all the beauty standards is a nightmare,
but why do we care?
Blind people they fall in love,
it's about how that person makes them feel,
so maybe beauty inside is real,
One day we become old and grey
so maybe how we are now is okay,
we won't think about the things we needed to change,
just thinking about the things we had to rearrange,
Because we didn't like the way that we looked.
Cancelled all those holidays that were booked.
Make memories, have fun, go out in your bikini in the sun.
Don't feel like you have to go for a morning run.
Your perfect the way you are,
Perfect skin? Flat belly?
Beauty? Set yourself free from society standards.
You'll never be perfect which is hard to accept
I may not have any beauty but I am me,
not so perfect, not fitting beauty standards me.

Neural pathways

I know you feel too broken to heal,
You think this is all you're cut out to be,
that your childhood trauma
is so ingrained in you
That it's just become your identity,
You think well everyone has moved on with their life's
Maybe the problem is just me,
Your self destructiveness, mood going up and down
Thoughts and memories replaying in your head
making you feel as if you will drown,
Your Brain was developing when the trauma happened,
The environment you grew up in your brain adapted
to help you cope.
Being hyper vigilant, a people pleaser
but that doesn't mean there is no hope,
A child that grew up in a unhealthy environment
would set their surroundings on fire just to be kept warm,
Picking up the broken pieces and moving them away after the storm,
thinking the pathway will always be messy and that is the norm,
Your basic needs weren't met
love care was what you were meant to get,
You deserved that ever since you grew in the womb
you deserved that when you had your first ever cry in the labour room,
It is more than possible to feel different,
for things to be different,
You are more than broken parts
in fact despite all you've been through
you have one of the biggest hearts,
Your brain adapted to survive,
But having the coping mechanisms you learnt later on
can make it harder to thrive,
although trauma is hard to overcome
your brain will always continue to create new neural pathways
as your begin to adapt existing ones
To the new environment you are in
and to not always let your negative thoughts win,
You can learn that you can set boundaries and it be okay
You can learn a missed phone call just means they're busy
And haven't left or gone away,
Where you are not living in constant anxiety or fear,
Where you get to the point you appreciate still being here,
Still being alive And you live rather than just survive,
you begin to grow as you start to know,
That things can be different,

you can be different that all the things you are facing you can overcome
and rewire your brain and neural pathways with new ones
You can still create a very beautiful life for yourself.

Never stop writing

You are and always will be the main character in your story,
In other peoples you may be a hero or maybe a villain,
May be in some you're admirable, in others you're totally oblivion,
You can't change the chapters that have already been written
But what I need you to understand is the rest of your story
is somewhat in your hands,
Not only are you the main character you are the author,
How would you like your story to end?
The last sentence to be?
Happy or full of misery?
Life will never be easy,
How do you want your story to end?
because it will one day,
But you're more than happy for your story to end now
because you can't see things ever being okay.
As a kid you had dreams and planned out your story
but it never turned out the way you planned it to,
Having so many battles you had to get through
When no one even knew,
But one day all the pain and hurt you feel will subside,
there will be a time you will read your story
chapter by chapter, line by line
Your story will become someone else's survival guide,
We never know what's around the bend,
Your story doesn't need to end,
maybe the chapter you're in does,
A fresh chapter a new start,
don't listen to your mind, listen to your heart,
It maybe a hard, messy, exhausting, beautiful story,
But take it in all of its glory,
It's your story to keep,
Make it unique, and never stop writing.

The greatest gift

Do you know what the greatest gift you can give to others is?
It's your happiness,
No not making them happy
But making you happy,
It's such a beautiful thing to witness,
When someone has struggled for so long seeing them carry on
And overtime seeing in themselves feel a little more strong,
Where they hit rock bottom but they've used that as a foundation to grow,
They got up everyday put on a smile even when they felt so low,
Despite all those battles they got through
There smile is still so bright,
Were they never of imagined they could make it through the night
But they get to the point where everyday isn't a complete and utter fight
They smile, they haven't smiled like this in a while,
They haven't smiled like this in a long time
But it isn't because they are pretending to be fine,
Seeing someone who wanted to give up and was in so much pain
But seeing them then,
Fall in love with life again,
You just look at them and you are so proud,
They fought even when the voices were so loud,
There smile lights everyone around
They were lost and now they're found,
Maybe not today or tomorrow or next week
but one day you'll be able to say you made it
And you will be glad that you didn't quit.

I'm sorry

I'm sorry that the world has treated you so badly
that it's made you feel like you no longer want to be in it,
I'm sorry that your head has drove you to destruction
Feeling as if you have no other choice but to quit,
People always tell you to talk about what you are going through,
But then you do
But they say your 'making it up' 'you're attention seeking'
but if only they knew,
So you decided to keep it all in
Hide all the pain and your suffering With a grin,
Waking up fighting everyday trying to not let the thoughts win
A unsuccessful suicide is attention seeking and not genuine
A successful suicide is a catastrophe,
That's the message given by society,
Who clearly don't know what it's like to suffer with suicidal ideation,
depression and anxiety,
What they tell you is 'well if you wanted to not be here you wouldn't be.'
Little do they know is everyday you want to be free,
What they don't tell you is you can be suicidal and still be here,
not acting on urges,
Still be alive, Just trying to survive,
Your feelings they invalidate,
Feeling as if your pain you have to demonstrate,
What they don't tell you is your presence
is the greatest present you can give to the earth,
That you haven't met everyone
who will love you for you and see your worth,
So as much as I know that you want to let go
You still being here will always be more beautiful
than the sunset your loved ones will see the next day,
The day after you got taken away So I know you're in pain,
After all the darkness you think you will never be the same
A world without you wouldn't feel right,
I know the thoughts make you wonder
if you will make it through the night But just hang on tight,
I know your mind is like living in a prison
But you will find someone who will listen
It's not weak to speak about all you are going through
And incase no one has said this,
I am so proud of you

I never want to stop grieving.

I never want to stop grieving for the people that I lost,
They say loving someone comes with a cost,
That person will be gone one day,
But we all know the consequences of loving someone
but we love anyway
I never want to stop grieving
even though my heart will always ache from them leaving
Because grief is just love with no place to go,
Grief is all the unexpressed love for them that I didn't let them know,
Although I will never again see there smile,
There voice in time I will start to forget for awhile,
We will never truly be apart
because no matter how much time passes
they will always be in my heart,
when it's a beautiful sky I will try not to cry,
the sky will always look more beautiful now
someone you love has flown up high,
I know it will be them when there's a white feather on the floor,
A little message that they are watching and there
when I thought I couldn't do this life thing without them anymore,
I will always hold a piece of them with me,
I just hope where ever they are they are at peace and are free
I hope now they're not in pain,
But life without them now will never be the same.

Sit with me for awhile.

Sit with me for awhile,
I know I will tell you to go away,
But I actually want you to stay,
Sit with me for awhile,
I know all day I have put on a smile,
But I can't find the words to say
That I am not okay,
And plus you probably wouldn't believe me anyway,
Sit with me for awhile,
Because I don't want to deal with this alone,
I feel like a prisoner in my own home
Sit with me for awhile,
Life feels like a chore, I have loads of laundry on the floor
In a pile,
please sit with me for awhile,
Just for a minute so I know someone is there
So my pain I can share,
So just sit with me for awhile,
I will act tough and tell you I need no one
But we all do,
You never know what anyone is truly going through,
So sit with me for awhile,
You'll say Stop trying to be brave I know your breaking inside,
I know your pain you're trying to hide,
Soon enough you will see the girl I try to be isn't me,
My thoughts are loud I'm alone in a crowd please sit with me for awhile
Not to take the pain away or make everything okay
Just sit with me for a little while.

You're an important part

Have you ever questioned your worth on this earth?
Have you ever thought no one would care if you're no longer there?
That you could disappear off the face of the earth tomorrow
and there would be no sorrow,
That it would just be another day,
everyone would be okay,
and all the pain and hurt you felt will just fade away.
You think your existence doesn't matter,
You think your crazy, I'm afraid so you're entirely bonkers
but I'll tell you a secret: all the best people are.
Those were the words of the mad hatter,
You are an important part,
and there will always be hope and light
as long as you have a beating heart,
What If you were to stay?
And one day you wake up and there's a little colour
instead of it all being grey.
What If this isn't all it'll be.
What If there is a way to escape misery.
Yes things may be bad,
but maybe one day you'll wake up and be glad.
That you pushed through, even though you didn't have a clue how too.
Of course your worth on this earth is large.
You have to take charge.
Yes, life isn't all rainbows and sunshine.
And sometimes it's easier to cover all the pain and upset with I'm fines.
You don't deserve to disappear and people are glad that you're still here.
So keep fighting, it's okay to let the light in.
Even if it seems frightening.

<u>What are you really hungry for?</u>

The narrative about struggling with an eating disorder,
Is you don't eat, you hate food, and it's all about weight,
Which makes suffers feel as if they're unable or undeserving
or invalidated to get help until
It can potentially be to late,
But what I want to talk about is hunger,
But not the type of hunger that you're probably thinking about,
People with eating disorders have to figure it out,
Where is the hunger coming from?
And what are they hungry for?
and this is probably something they've never had to think about before
Most of the time people are hungry because of unmet needs,
People who binge do that to fill the loneliness
they feel inside and for comfort
And is nothing to do with greed,
The person who may want to be the skinniest version of themselves,
May not just think they're fat, it may not be anything to do with that,
Maybe they just wanted to be looked after
the way you're meant to when you are small,
Without being Ill they don't believe they are loveable,
Some may of not had a enough nurture and care and affection
Some are hungry for perfection,
Some are hungry for control,
When you've struggled with an eating disorder for a long time
It can feel like an eating disorder is all you are as a whole,
An eating disorder can provide a purpose
And for some reason finally feeling a sense that you belong
Even if deep down you know what you're doing is wrong.
An eating disorder isn't a weight disorder it's a psychological one
And just because someone is eating or doesn't fit the narrative
of what an eating disorder is considered to be
doesn't mean they are free and they're still having battles to overcome,
So suffers may have to ask themselves a question
they probably haven't before
What are they really hungry for?

You are loved

Their inability to love you the way you deserved to be loved
is not your fault.
Doesn't mean you're hard to love and no one can ever love you.
Just because they didn't do the job they were meant to.
Doesn't mean it was you,
Sometimes the person who was meant to or we wanted to love us don't
But that doesn't mean everybody won't.
And now you've created this guard that's hard to break down,
To scared to let it down
because you think nobody can turn all that hurt pain and Grief around
You haven't been loved the way that you should
Now you question if anyone ever could
You push people away but let me tell you something,
You are okay.
There's always someone out there that does
and will care even if care now gives you a little scare.
You aren't hard to love. It wasn't you.
Just because you don't really like who you are doesn't
mean everyone else will hate you too.
You are loved, you are enough
Let people in because there are people out there
who want to see you win.

Who are you?

Everyone's going to have a different story to who you are.
So you shouldn't let what people think get in the way of you going far.
Your story so far may have been sadness, pain and upset.
But there's so much things you have to experience yet,
Your life is just as important as others,
You don't have to hide from the world under the covers,
You have to decide what the story is for yourself,
and forget about everyone else.
You don't think there's a way out this is all you've known,
Maybe you're too scared to step out of your comfort zone,
Being sad and in pain your whole life is a scary story
You can be different if you want different
Don't let anyone take away your glory.
It's not easy but hopefully in time the pain will feel less and less,
Don't let anyone knock your progress,
No matter how big or small you did it, yes you did it all,
A friend said to me there's doing something
'when it feels wrong' and that's called bravery.
And you are being brave if you're doing something that makes you afraid,
You get to decide how your story is going to be but first
you have to set yourself free,
From people's opinions, expectations, perceptions.
And start living the life you want to live.
It's your story, so never let anyone take away your glory.

<u>Perspective of a paramedic-</u>

(in honour of all the paramedics.)
Blue lights in the dark
We never run out of spaces to park
We are paramedics,
We stop the bleeding, and help those who are needing.
Sirens get pressed,
Family and friends of the patients are blessed,
We calm them down and reassure them when they feel stressed.
Each shift putting on the green uniform, ready to face the storm,
Ready for the CPR we may or may not have to perform,
Defibrillator charged ready for cardiac arrests,
We as paramedics will always do our best,
Everyday putting us to the test,
Heart attacks collapses, brain injuries and falls
We go to every call no matter how small,
To keep patients alive, because they deserve a great life,
If someone gets stabbed don't pull out the knife.
This job is rewarding,
999 whats your emergency I used to always have recording.
Now my dream has finally come true.
Helping others get through pressing the siren that's blue.
Whilst learning how to stop someone else's bleeding
I unintentionally learnt how to stop my own.
With every call I go to I don't want the patient to feel alone.
My uniform on, my hair in braids.
Knowing that I did this. I did this. Not just the grades on a page.
Excited but Scared and nervous for each call out there is no doubt.
But I need to be braving.
As soon as I enter that van. Shut the doors
There will be millions of lives that need saving.
From cannulating or a pulse that needs locating.
We will press the blue light, and your life
we will fight and be on our way to try and save the day.
Blue lights in the dark to help you through
All you need to do is look out for a light and siren that's blue.

Million reasons to stay

When you have a million reasons to let go,
There will always be a million and one reasons to stay.
Although I know it doesn't seem that way.
Right now you're in the dark.
Mental illness doesn't make you crazy
weak or mean you're a person with lots of broken parts.
Maybe a reason to stay is for all the sunsets you have left to see
Or jumping out of the aeroplane and it feels like you're flying free.
Maybe a reason to stay is for others.
Or those days watching tv shows
while it's cold outside under the covers.
Maybe it's taking a walk in the autumn leaves.
Or maybe it's seeing something and it makes
you smile or laugh even if it's brief.
You're yet to see your favourite movie
that you don't even know exists yet.
And your favourite song,
How about you prove everyone that doubted you wrong.
You don't get another life you only get one
And I know you feel these battles you can't overcome.
But remember when you have a million reasons to let go
There will always be a million and one reasons to stay,
Right now you're in the grey but one day you will be okay.

Thought and fact

You know not everything your mind tells you is the truth,
you say it is but where is your proof?
Your depression and cruel mind wants you to stay where you are
it doesn't want you to go far.
To be honest ,harsh but true but some disorder
won't stop till your dead
but I know how hard it is to fight for another life instead.
And I know with depression it's easier to fake a smile.
Even when you haven't felt truly happy in a while.
When I struggled, my mind convinced me of terrible things,
that people were saying terrible things
but actually those people wanted to see me so desperately win
I got told my head can lie to me,
but I didn't believe a life without pain could be achieved.
It's hard to deal with the intrusive thoughts
that come in your mind at random times
That isn't that kind.
Opinions don't define your reality but they can impact your mentality.
How can our head not be right?
Truth is depression, eating disorders,
mental illnesses you need to fight
and it's hard when you can't see the light
Your head is giving you a fright
Sometimes actions have to come before motivation,
which takes dedication
Our head can be our worst enemy
but believe me you won't always be trapped one day you'll be free.
Not everything your head tells you is true
I wish this was something a long time ago I knew.
Don't believe everything your head is telling you.
Your head wants you to stay where you are
go Against it and you could go far.

Weather in our heads

Sometimes we may wake up and the day before it said it was sun.
So we wake up and expect to have fun.
But sometimes we expect sun then it rains.
Having to stay indoors, thoughts ticking in our brains.
This can be like the emotions, happy and sad.
Waking up to a little less rain, a little less pain. We will be glad.
We go to sleep not knowing how we will feel the next day.
Not knowing if we will wake up feeling okay.
It's like the weather not knowing if it'll be cloudy or sunny.
Or will we be okay or in pain.
Never knowing that never.
But I guess that's just life though
Trying to get through the high and the lows.
We can't predict how we are going to feel in the next minute
or in the next day or in the next month.
Yet we live in a state of fear with the future being unclear.
With people asking us where do you see yourself in 5 years?
We can't answer that.
Things happen that's out of our control.
Like weather tomorrow it'll rain or the sun will shine.
Whether we wake up in pain or we will wake up fine.
But we just wake up and see on the day
Hoping that we will be okay.
It doesn't have to be too sunny or too bright.
Just enough so we don't have to put so much energy into fight.
Not too much rain, not too much pain.
The weather is like our emotions I'm trying to explain.
Like the weather.
The rain does pass. So hopefully that means the pain won't last.

Eating disorder

An eating disorder isn't an Instagram trend
It isn't always having avocado on toast
An eating disorder makes you push away the people you love the most,
It's not always being skin and bone
If an eating disorder was a person
they would have a heart of stone,
An eating disorder will take everything away
from you till you have nothing left
But it convinces you a life with an eating disorder is the best,
It will convince you of that till you're very last breath,
An eating disorder will want more and more
and it will never be good enough
until it reaches the point of death,
People are not healed just because they're weight restored,
They still need to be reassured,
That it's what the body needs and it's nothing to do with greed
People are not healed or not suffering
just because they may be considered a healthy weight,
We need to let go of that narrative
as it makes suffers believe they're not worthy of help
until it's too late,
It's not always crying over a meal
It's not about what we eat
It's about how it makes us feel
An eating disorder is one of the hardest illnesses to beat
And the battle isn't over just because people eat,
An eating disorder captures the person
you are till your turned into this shell
Mental illness doesn't have a look,
you can't see a person and tell that they're unwell
Living with an eating disorder is living with a bully that won't go away
It says it won't till you obey,
Living with restrictions and rules
Fighting an illness that is cruel,
So no an eating disorder isn't a trend
Most people with eating disorders have trauma
and are just trying to recover and mend

Stick around.

We are all trying to get through this life thing,
sometimes we lose, sometimes we win,
no amount of anxiety will change the future,
Because we can never be sure to what the future will bring,
But even if you're in pain and it seems nothing is changing
And it just stays the same,
Even if life keeps knocking you down to the ground
Maybe it's still worth sticking around,
No one really knows what they're doing in life
but we wake up and carry on and try
Anyone that says they 100% know exactly what they are doing in life
are probably telling a lie
But we have a lifetime to learn what it's all about
and it's okay if it takes awhile to figure it all out,
but I know it feels easier to give up,
sometimes it's easier to pretend you're fine
I know you feel like a burden
and you have no idea how you're going to get through
But I promise no one will be better off without you
For the rest of their existence people will be sad
and I am not saying this to make you feel bad,
But one day you may be glad that you never gave up
But we can't wait till it magically goes away
We have to fight,
We have to fight every single day,
You will be okay.

Driving on foggy morning

Navigating your way through life
while suffering with depression and mental health
is like trying to drive a car on a foggy morning,
Depression is an abductor that takes people hostage,
Depression is a cruel and evil thing
that will never stop it's lies and manipulation till it wins,
Depression sucks the life out of you
And the loneliest part about it all is
no one will ever know what you are going through,
Where getting out of bed is the hardest thing to do
But you just about 'function' because you have no choice but to
Depression is not a friend but it convinced you it is
Because at times it can feel safe and scary to let go of
Sometimes depression can feel like a friend
And all you want and wish for is the pain to end
Depression is devastating and lonely,
And no one will ever be able to fully comprehend
how deliberating depression can really be.
Because the things with mental health you cannot see
because a face of depression is not always full of misery,
depression deprives you of the ability to have hope
Which is why when suffering with depression
it makes it much more difficult to cope,
Depression isn't just about feeling sad or blue,
It can be feeling empty and numb too,
People with depression are always trying to keep it Together
Dealing with depression is more than just feeling under the weather,
For the black cloud to lift we crave
Getting through the day requires being really brave
We just need love and care and someone to be there
Somewhere in us is the person we used to be,
We are just struggling with an Illness that you cannot see.

what i wish you knew.

When struggling with an eating disorder or
disordered eating there's always one thing I wish people would just know,
So I didn't have to feel alone,
and feel as if I'm facing this battle all on my own,
Just because I may eat it doesn't mean I'm okay,
But to everyone else around me it seems that way,
But If we were to change the topic to an alcoholic who has stopped drinking,
They still haven't really changed there way of thinking
They still have the problem, the urge to drink and the reason to why
they started in the first place
It's a very scary space to be,
It can start off with feeling as if it's the only thing I can control
But then very soon it starts to control me,
It can numb us and distract us from how we really feel,
But apparently to feel is the only way we are going to truly heal,
Maybe it gives some people a purpose a sense that they belong
Because without it they don't feel enough,
Letting go of it can feel wrong
We convince ourself doing the opposite to what our heads says is weak
but listening to what are head says is strong
But if we listen to our heads we wouldn't be around for very long,
But that's what it wants,
We think we are never enough
But it will never be enough
It will always want more and more till it brings us to the floor
feeling as if we can't take much anymore,
We just wanted to feel okay,
We never meant for things to turn out this way,
We lose ourselves, we can potentially affect our health,
So Just because We are doing what is needed it
doesn't mean we want to or that it is easy or that anything is better
In fact we convince ourselves we are not Ill enough yet
But how ill will we get?
Till we realise to our surprise
The eating disorder is not our friend but our enemy
And our eating disorder won't let us go,
So it's only us that can let go and break free
But we convince ourselves that it makes us happy,
It's like a toxic abusive relationship,
It's so hard to leave but once we do it's easier to breathe.

Don't end your life today

Don't end your life today because
There's movies that you haven't even seen
Don't end your life today,
Because there so many places that you've never been,
Don't end your life today,
Because you still have so many times
when you can lick the spoon when baking
Don't end your life today,
Because you have no idea how many life's your making,
whilst you are simply breaking,
Don't end your life today
Because you still can see so many sun rises and sun sets
Don't end your life today because
You haven't experienced the best day of your life yet
Don't end your life today because
Your dog your cat will wonder why you went away
Your family and friends will wonder what they could
have done to have made you stay
One more day one more chance
This is about staying alive long enough till it's no longer a question
Till the thought of waking up tomorrow
May bring you excitement instead of sorrow,
So don't end your life today because
Starbucks and Costa will always have your favourite drink
at Christmas time
Don't end your life today
Because no, no nobody will be fine
The world may carry on,
But a world without you would just feel so wrong,
So don't end your life today
Because remember when you never thought
you'd get through the worst day of your life but you did
Don't end your life today,
Because maybe in the future you will have a little kid
Don't end your life today,
Because your story one day could be someone else's survival guide
All because you simply tried,
To show others to choose life over suicide
Don't end your life today,
Survive, do so much more than that be alive
Your feelings will pass, nothing lasts
And you may feel pain again
But you will be able to learn to find a way to cope

In the time you feel despair,
Others have hope,
So although my reasons to not end your life today
may seem pointless
to you right now
Anything that may save your life is worth saying
There is always someone praying that the light will come on
That you stay strong
Because you belong
So don't end your life
Don't end it today,
Don't end it tomorrow,
Don't end it ever,
No matter how alone you feel we are all in this together

When all you've known is grey

How do you imagine the look of colour
when your whole life all you have seen is grey?
How do you picture a day or a time where things are actually okay
When all you've known is pain?
No matter the hard work you put in
it all just stays the same,
Sometimes mental illness doesn't want to set us free,
We resign to the fact that maybe just maybe this is our reality,
How do you imagine a life when an illness or disorder
has always been in the centre of your life?
Your fearful of strife
To scared to let go of what you know
So you stay in the grey
Because you almost become okay with not being okay
And attached to the feeling,
That staying in the dark in a weird way sounds appealing
Or at least it's easier then healing
To essentially let go of a part of you that taught you how to survive
Because although the behaviours are self destructive and damaging
Somehow we think they help us be alive
To cope with the things we are unable to
Because in that moment maybe it was the only thing
that could help us get through,
Sometimes it's easier to stay where we are
because what if We put all that work and go far
For it to only get bad again
What then?
Maybe a life with illness brings safety
And familiarity,
We also may think it brings us clarity
But sometimes we can't just stay in our comfort zone,
We have to step out even if we are stepping out into the unknown
Because although you may not be able to imagine the look of colour
because you are so used to the grey,
It may get bad again at some point but that's okay
This may not be it,
But it will be if you quit,
There's good amongst the chaos
You have a whole life time
To learn how to be more than just fine

No shame

There is no shame in asking for help when it's needed
But it would be a real shame to lose you,
I know right now it doesn't feel like you're going to make it through,
Or even if you want to,
But your life is really precious and worth saving
I know it's not really about dying
It's the peace
it's the pain to fade away that
you're craving
I promise no one is angry with you
It's just sometimes
anger can come out as fear or because they care
and they don't want you to go
and there scared that they can't get you to stay,
They want to tell you it's going to be okay
But the depression is so strong it doesn't care what others have to say,
It convinces you that it's always going to be this way,
But you have survived 100% of your worst days
Even if it was just about,
I know you're exhausted and you just want a way out
But one day the pain won't be as Heavy
Because I promise you this isn't it
And one day you will be grateful that you didn't quit
Maybe it won't be today or tomorrow
Maybe it will be a few years from now,
But it will get easier somehow,
I know you are tired but you can lean on others if that is required
But please try to hold on a little longer
Because Eventually you will get stronger
There is no shame in asking for help,
But it would be such a shame to lose you.

accountability

I saw a message that said
You can't wait until life isn't hard anymore to be happy,
I lay in bed I listen to my head
and wait to not be sad
but for as long as I can remember things have been bad
People tell me I need to take accountability
and when I first got told that,
I thought they were making out that this is a choice
and that this whole thing is easy
But it isn't,
But it is about saying enough is enough, yes it's tough
But I've got to get myself out of this rut I am in
and I can't keep letting my head win
You have to try and be consistent
because one slip up you risk falling down the hole
again with your head driving you insane
but it's so hard to fight constantly and the hardest
part it doesn't just get better instantly
I need to try and remember that
I can't wait for life not to be hard anymore,
Some days it looks like brushing my teeth
while sitting down on the bathroom floor,
Or sometimes it's feeling like this relentless cycle is never going to end,
Sometimes it's playing pretend
But we have to do the hard thing anyway,
And just hope that eventually things will be okay,
It's okay If you don't wake up until 2pm
but it's better to do something than nothing at all,
It's better to do something even if it's small
Being productive looks different on everyone,
Everyone is facing battles they are trying to overcome
So if all you did today was survive then that's enough,
Some days will be easier and some days are tough
But you can't wait till life isn't hard anymore
You have to keep fighting,
even if it feels like you have nothing that's worth fighting for
You will always be worth saving in someone's eyes,
so it's always worth waking up and giving this life thing a try.

Little me

There was once a little girl,
Someone you may know.
She had a beautiful smile.
And lovely hair that she'd been growing for a while.
She stands against the measuring wall
And stood tall, proudly shown how much she had grown.
When she falls over she stands back up
Even though her leg she cut
She had a little graze and she was so brave
so she just carried on and went to play.
She was perfect in every single way.
There was a much older girl standing in looking in the mirror
and the little girl I explained at the beginning was near her.
This older girl thought she was ugly and no good,
that no one would ever love her even if they could.
Her face full of ache her thighs full of stretch marks.
Little did she know beauty came from the heart.
The older girl and little girl were standing in the mirror
and what the little girl said couldn't be any clearer.
The little girl said what is wrong with me?
because I am just the girl that You used to be.
Am I ugly? Am I no good?
Maybe I'll change the way I look if you think I should?
The older girl says no there's nothing wrong with you.
The little girl says there's nothing wrong with you too
In fact you were one who helped me get through
, you were the one who taught me to be brave when I was so afraid.
The little girl said she's got to go now but before she left
She said Can I say one last thing if you allow?
The older girl said yes she wouldn't say anything less,
The little girl said sometimes in life you may get knocked down
if you fall you just have to stand tall,
and if your knees you've grazed you've just got to be brave.

Eat, forget, repeat

Yeah I lost weight
But I lost other things to,
I thought it made me happy but I don't know if that's true,
Maybe for a little while,
Till eventually I lost my smile
People lost trust in me
Eventually it feels like an illness becomes your identity
Yeah I lost weight,
But I thought I was okay because I ate,
I lost the person i used to be
but I couldn't stop because the damage
I was doing to myself I couldn't see ,
I was filled with anxiety trying to fit in with society
I wasn't doing it to be the girls in magazines
I wasn't doing it to be like the models you see on tv screens
I was doing it as it was something I could control
But eventually you spiral down this hole,
I did it because I didn't know what else to do,
It was a coping mechanism to help me
when I'm finding things difficult to get through,
Even though it was my way to cope
I lost hope
I lost my personality
I lost The capacity to think about other things
I missed out on making memories
I lost weight but above everything else I lost my self
I may never be the girl I used to be
but I have to learn being ill isn't my identity
Recovery is about discovery
Sometimes getting better is scary
It makes us weary
But I lost so much I guess I can't lose anything else
I just don't want to lose myself,
Not again
Which means I can't keep doing the same
Maybe present me may not want it
But maybe future me will be glad I didn't quit
Eat, forget, repeat
Maybe eventually this thing I'll beat.

Recovery

For me I felt like getting better was a scary thing,
As I guess I was unsure what recovery can bring but
one thing I know is if I let go
I will run the risk of getting hurt again,
And what do I do then?
I found comfort in my darkness because
For as long as I can remember I've been in pain,
So I may as-well just stay the same,
Because then I won't fall down that way,
But even in the darkest times there will always be moments
where it's less grey,
And if you stay where you are
, you really will never experience things being okay,
But mental illness or not,
life is very up and down,
One day you'll smile, the next you may frown,
What's the point in getting better for it to at some point again get bad
Because well your existence in life isn't to just be sad,
Being sad isn't all you are or all you will be,
it's just sometimes getting better isn't easy,
When you feel like you can't keep going it isn't a sign
for you to give up it means you just have to try something else,
Every step you take be proud of yourself,
Do the scary thing,
Even if you're unsure to what recovery will bring,
do the scary thing and don't let mental illness win,
Although it may not feel like it,
you are bigger than the demons in your head,
And there is nothing bad about saying,
Do you know what this isn't working?
I'm going to try something else.

The world went quiet

The next day was the day the world went quiet,
Lots of flowers from where you took your own life
laying from blue to violet,
The next day was the day your sisters are without a sibling,
Your mum and dad searching through all your old things,
The next day was the day they played your favourite song,
Feeling guilty because they thought you were okay,
but they were wrong,
The next day was the day everyone's life would change forever,
When they realise you are now gone
and will never be able to spend time together,
The next day was the day where everyone was in disbelief,
trying to find ways to deal with the grief
the next day was the day they would never again hear your voice
they missed your cheeky smile,
they would instantly bring you back if they had the choice,
the next day was grey, no one was happy to see you had gone away,
In fact they wished you would have stayed,
they knew you wanted the pain to end,
and none of what you was going through
was easy they aren't going to pretend
This isn't a guilt trip just saying people do care,
whether you stay or go and I wanted you to know
we will all die one day
Just please choose to stay and don't let it be today.

medication

A cancer patient needs chemo
and we would never call them weak for needing that,
A person with a heart condition may need medication
and we never call them weak or deny them of that,
Physical illness and mental illness are the same
the only difference is the organ that is being impacted,
Mental illness is the chemical Imbalance in our brains,
Why should we deny ourselves of help,
because we think it isn't that bad,
'Oh don't worry I'm just a little bit sad'
We completely invalidate how deliberating mental illness can be,
Simply because mental illness we cannot see,
We don't wait to receive help only when the cancer becomes terminal
The effects of mental illness
Can be completely irreversible,
So taking medication for our mental health
shouldn't be seen as anything other then treating an organ
in our body to work a certain way,
There's nothing wrong with taking meds to feel slightly more okay,
There should be no shame
in trying to help deal with what's going on in our brain,
In fact when someone with cancer goes through treatment
we see them as brave,
And strong,
And I think the same goes when someone with mental illness
Goes through recovery and decides to carry on.

one amazing you.

What if everyone doesn't actually hate you,
What if the intrusive thoughts aren't actually true
If only you knew,
If only you knew that when you smile it makes others smile to,
Especially if you haven't had a smile for awhile,
That your laugh brings laughter to those all around,
That even when you were lost,
You helped someone else to be found,
That you make someone's day a little less grey,
If only you knew that all people want is for you to be okay,
That there's someone who's up at night hoping you choose to stay,
If only you knew people do care,
and there is someone there,
That you make the world a better place simply by still being here,
That a life you can't imagine right now is on the other side of fear,
You are loved even on days you don't love yourself,
You are loved even on days you feel sadness and nothing else,
Just because you may not like yourself very much,
doesn't mean everyone else hates you to,
there maybe 7.8 billion people in the world
but there's only one unique and amazing you.

Will I wait?

Will I wait?
I debate,
Will I wait or
Will it be too late?
Will I wait?
Will I wait till I feel ready?
Will I wait till things in my life feel more steady?
Will I be in my nursing home worrying that
they put sugar in my tea?
Or anxiously waiting because they should have
brought my snack at three,
Will I regret waiting?
Will I regret debating?
The decision to let go of what I know?
To hold on because letting go of something
that people told me was destroying
me felt wrong,
Will I regret the calories in the bowl of pasta
that I don't even remember?
Or will I regret not choosing recovery
When I thought I should have done one September?
Will I live my life in fear year after year?
Using my sweater at dinner time to wipe away my tears?
Will I let this go round and round
to the point it makes me so miserable and constantly
drags me to the ground?
Will I wait for the perfect day
And I feel ready to conquer my fears?
Or will I start making the changes right now,right here?
Will I wait for the perfect day or will I just obey?
Or will I feel the fear, will I feel horrible and do it anyway?
Will I let life go on around me?
Or will I fight my hardest to try and be free
Will I wait?
Or will it become too late?

Butterfly.

When I'm feeling down I look to the ground
but I remember the butterflies fly high in the sky,
When I want to give up, I see one and remember
I've just got to try,
Because they talk about the caterpillar when it's in its nest,
then to it's best but they fail to mention the rest,
They don't just get up spread their wings and go,
Although that is the story we all know,
But that isn't how they grow,
They dissolve into this lump of goo,
And they seem so trapped,
it doesn't look like or seem like they are going to ever make it through
But they do,
Because that's the process,
First they have to be a mess,
Before they can spread their wings and fly,
So it's why it's important when you want to give up that you don't,
You always get up and try,
it's okay to take a rest in that little nest,
But remember when the butterfly is cooped in it's goo
and they feel in isolation,
and alone that's when they grow their wings
and make their way home,
The butterfly's always gets to a point where they think it's over,
But one day when they be strong enough they burst there way through the goo
and they never knew,
They would be able to spread their wings
but they did and that was their closure,
They learnt to fly because they gave it another try,
We never know the changes the butterfly has to achieve,
We just believe the butterfly was always like that,
But it's gone through a lot and this is the beauty it became
You can do the same,
No matter the weather through the sun and the rain,
So If your trapped in the goo,
Remember The butterfly and you will be able to fly one day too.

When food wasn't the enemy.

As a kid I would run around a soft play,
we would then go to the table where they would lay
a jug of orange and black currant juice,
and we would all down one or two glasses to take the thirst away,
As a kid on my birthday,
I couldn't wait for them all to finish singing ,
with the cake so we could all sit and have a slice,
But now having a slice comes with a price,
Hearing the man in the ice cream van then sitting outside,
When I ate the ice cream I never once cried,
but then it all changed which seemed strange,
How something that once brang me joy now brings me worry and doubt,
and I never quite knew what that was all about,
Now food is the enemy that locks me in a cage filled with misery
Wondering if I'll ever be set free,
Will I one day be able to not use my plate to demonstrate
the pain that I'm in,
Will I let the demons win? Will I ever be that little girl?
Who ate a piece of cake
who never once thought eating it was a mistake?
Will I ever be the girl again who loved cheese
if someone said if she wanted chicken nuggets from McDonald's
she'd say yes please
On the first of December eating a little piece of chocolate before school
Well that was If I didn't eat them all,
Or sitting out in the sun having those milk lollies on a school trip
Never once concerned about the Calories touching my lip,
I would pretend to have shots by drinking the drink from the lid,
These were all the little things I did as a kid,
But maybe one day I'll be sat in the sun,
and this battle I would have overcome,
Having a hot chocolate on a winter's day
and accepting and knowing that that is okay
Because In years time you won't remember the calories
in the bowl of pasta you ate
You would want to look back and think about the memories
that you made and think wow that was great,
And it's not easy but there can be good times
It's been said to feel the fear and do it anyway
If you relate to what I have to say,
Then I hope one day things start to become okay,

Once we learn we don't need to listen to that little voice or obey,
Maybe present you won't Thank-you for it but future you may,
It's fine to fight the demons, it's going to be okay!

Being Ill isn't our identity.

I am scared of people thinking I am okay even if I am,
Scared they will just go away
As if being ill is my identity,
that if I wasn't then no one will love or care for me,
But apparently that isn't true
and I am not the only one that feels that way others do to,
Some people illicit care through illness,
scared if they let go no one will be there,
They don't believe they are enough to care about without it,
It keeps them trapped from knowing that they are more than enough
Just by being who they are,
That actually people are rooting for them and wanting them to go far,
The people that matter will still be there and will still care,
And actually being well and happy
would be the greatest gift they could give to others
Whenever I made a step forward people told me they were proud of me
that's because doing something that feels wrong isn't weak it's bravery,
Maybe the care you received when you were young wasn't enough
But you are enough and you have suffered enough,
Risks need to be taken to learn
we are mistaken that being ill is all we are or all we will have to be
Because being ill isn't are identity.

Tiny victories.

Celebrate the tiny victories,
because one day they will turn into something bigger and better,
We should celebrate our victories,
no matter what the size,
how much those tiny things add up in the end you would be surprised,
You may not know it yet but you know that moment,
that moment where everything slows down,
you look around and for so long you have been lost
but now you think to yourself I think I have been found,
It's those moments that matter, the now
Where you let your mind run free which is difficult to allow
But your not worrying about all the horrible things somehow,
The reason the now moment's matter the most is
because they are happening right before our eyes,
You have a smile a real smile,
and this all happened because you gave up or
thought you did for awhile but you gave things another try,
But now all that pain and suffering and hurt,
Those times you didn't think you could do it anymore,
It starts to become clear why you kept going for
As you know things now you never did before,
It doesn't matter how many moments you have,
sometimes the special thing about moments
is you don't know it until you look back on it,
How special they truly are
And you've seen yourself come so far,
It's not about the amount, it's about making those moments count.

Walk through the rain.

'Take whatever's coming at you as rain
and put your umbrella up and walk through it,'
Even when you want to quit,
I know it may feel like you don't have any value on this earth,
but you make people happier than they would be without you
I just wish you could afford to give some of that happiness to you too,
I know it may seem easier to just go,
You've never felt so low,
Things don't seem like they will ever be okay
but one day we will leave this earth anyway
So we may as-well stay.
You will laugh a million times
and you will also cry a million times but that's fine,
Stay alive today, stay alive tomorrow,
And keep coming back to this whenever you feel the need to go
and you feel alone,
Right now you're at rock bottom, 'life has to be lived to be understood',
it has to be lived to realise there are some good
and those moments will make it worth it,
You lost the will to live it can't get worse then that,
Choosing life means dealing with the things that you didn't want to
deal with in the first place,
but comes with the possibility of feeling things if were to leave this place,
and if you had chosen to not be here anymore,
Maybe after all this, things will be even better then they were before
Sometimes you not always going to be sure,
Sometimes it's about putting trust into others,
getting out of bed and out from under the covers to step into the world,
And eventually you will see colour,
So people will tell you to stay
because they know the grey will slowly fade away,
I know you want to be free but we tell you to stay
because we see a future you cannot see, I hope you choose life again,
Because the world is a better place because it has you,
You make a difference by simply being here if only you knew
Hold on for another minute,
This isn't going to be it,
This isn't all your life will be,
stay because we know there's a life out there that you cannot see
You are trapped in depression
And I hope one day depression sets you free
So you can be the person you want to be,
So grab that Umbrella and walk through the rain ,
I hope you are able to choose life again.

Your child doesn't owe you anything

This is for the parents,
The parents who think because they're your child they have to obey,
and do everything you say,
Your child doesn't owe you anything,
You're not loving or providing for your child to get something back in return
It's a job, it's a responsibility
Your love, your care, they shouldn't have to earn,
We are not dolls, robots or machines,
Don't let your child grow up with unmet needs,
Your child doesn't owe you good behaviour or good grades,
Making them feel like they are never good enough,
isn't how they should be raised,
Every achievement they achieve should be praised,
As a parent you have to step up,
you make mistakes but you own your mistakes
and grow and it's okay some things you're not going to know,
being a perfect text book parent isn't what this is about.
There's going to be times where you are stressed scared without a doubt,
The same way you're not going to know things
the same with your child one day they didn't know how to walk and talk,
They won't understand why you can't draw on a wall,
they may not get all A's at school.
They don't owe you respect,
respect is reciprocal,
Being a parent doesn't start when your child will remember things,
in fact it's key your there right when their life begins,
It's not about being a perfect parent,
all they want, all they need
is your love and care, for you to just simply be there,
Your child doesn't owe you anything,
Your behaviours, your feelings that's on you,
Don't put that on your kid because
they will spend the rest of their life
thinking that was because of something they did,
Maybe parents act or behave based on how they were treated
when they were young and there trauma
and although that's hard and it's not there fault
they are accountable in breaking the cycle going forward,
Your child doesn't owe you anything.

<u>Anxiety.</u>
They think anxiety is just being anxious,
but that's just a Symptom of anxiety,
There's not just one symptom there's a whole variety,
But there are loads of stereotypes that we need to break down as a society.
Anxiety,
anxiety is the crushing feeling on your chest,
making you feel like you can't breathe,
Anxiety makes you feel like all the negative feelings
you feel will never leave,
Anxiety makes you have self doubt
and back out on things
because you don't believe you are good enough to achieve,
It's the late night tossing and turning and trying to sleep,
It's like your is mind awake,
but your so tired from the many hours you sat and weeped,
It's looking at the time pass by and you can't shut off no matter how hard you
try,
It's counting down to three before you leave the front door,
because your knowing the day you're about to face and what's in store,
And I mean sometimes it wouldn't look like
I have anxiety because not much seems different from you and me,
But one minute I could feel as if I'm swimming the next it feels like I'm
drowning
But I take a minute and try to breathe,
Anxiety is thinking of the worst case scenario
in your head before it's even happened,
Which you know it's an unhelpful thought
because it leaves you even more scared,
But at least you can say to yourself
'Well at least I have prepared'
Anxiety is much more then rocking back and forth on the floor
Anxiety is a battle everyday,
Making you wonder if things are ever going to be okay,
And it's horrible to feel that way.

Self love

They talk about self love as if it's just about face masks
and looking in the mirror doing self talks and motivational speeches,
which is all well and good but that's not how I understood, self love.
I think self love for me is hard normally,
any kind of love towards myself I discard
but If you were asked what is self love what would you say?
Would it be where you see your flaws and accept them anyway?
That the way you are is okay?
Is self love realising your enough?
Is self love setting boundaries and saying no?
Is self love still caring for yourself even if you're feeling low?
Is self love finding and creating a home within yourself?
Is self love looking after your Health?
Is self love realising you're not any less deserving
of love and care than anyone else?
Is self love a thing you have to earn or a thing you have to learn?
we are our own worst enemy and maybe self love will set us free,
I am always going to be stuck with me,
so maybe if I can't love, I can accept
It may not be love but maybe I'll feel enough,
enough for me and not the person people expect me to be
I will be my own friend, not my own enemy.

Becoming me.

'Oh you've changed'
Which to me makes sense
But to others it seems strange,
'Where has the old you gone?'
Well she had to spend the majority of her time trying to be strong,
always putting a smile on,
Fighting silent battles that no one knew about,
Is it worth keeping on going, she never saw a way out,
And people would say well I don't see a problem you look okay?
Oh you're a survivor you just get through anything that comes your way,
As if the things I have been through make me tough
but let me tell you these last few years have been far from easy
they've been rough,
And sometimes I wish I could fall apart,
but no instead I walk around with a heavy heart,
Pouring my pain on a page, creating art
But none of this pain is poetic,
The words form gracefully into the page but I am still trapped in this cage
A cage they call mental illness,
So maybe I am not the girl I used to be
But pain and experiences changes you, you see,
And maybe in the future I'll be stronger for it,
But right now I don't want someone to tell me to be strong,
They'll look at me and tell me I belong
that all my head says is wrong
and actually they'll tell me it's okay not to be strong
for a little while that I can let go of the fake smiles,
It's okay to fall apart as long as you get back up
and carry on creating art for the people on this earth,
That right now you feel broken but that doesn't damage your worth
So I may not be the same as I used to be
But there will be a new me
And hopefully that new me will feel more free.

Dear myself,

As a kid, you were never really scared of monsters under the bed,
As you had bigger demons to face around you and in your head,
You were made to believe things about you
and the world that aren't true
You learnt to survive the only way you knew how to,
Right now you feel as if you are in a forest
With two paths to choose from,
But both feel scary no path will feel like you win
But both feel like you will lose, One way is the path you know,
Self-destructive painful and slow,
The other path is scary and painful too
A path you have never gone through,
Down that path,
you may stumble around in the darkness and lose yourself,
As you learn to realise you are not a number or diagnosis or symptoms,
you are someone else,
That was just a part of you,
that felt stuck to you like glue,
The path you know will always be the same
Horrible and being in pain but you're comfortable with that path
it became okay,
Whereas the other way leads to a different destination,
well that's what people say,
But it takes a lot of dedication to get there,
things may creep out of the corner which gives you a scare,
You may trip and fall, you may feel as if you can't do any of this at all,
You don't need to hate yourself,
and by the way, people will still love you even when you are in good health,
I know you don't feel like you deserve good,
And you don't feel like anyone gets you, you feel so misunderstood.
You're scared of things not working out
but you're scared of things working out too
Because you've never really lived a life with stability
and a life where things are slightly okay or even feeling happy will feel new,
People tell you, you are worth more than you know,
But you are too afraid to let all the pain and suffering go.
So which path to choose when both paths will feel like you will lose?
But what a great feeling it will be
When the light at the end of the darkness you will see,
When you walked the path you never walked before
When you continued walking despite not wanting to walk anymore,
I know you want to know what will happen In Life but none of us do
But that doesn't mean we have to protect ourselves
and put our walls up for the pain we may or may not go through,

I know you are scared but you can be scared and brave,
As you eventually walk out of the darkness
your loved ones there waiting and give you a cheer and a wave,
Finally feeling free and no longer scared is all you've ever craved.
So you're in a forest with two scary paths ahead,
Do you go down the path you normally go down
Or try a different one instead?
Because if not you then who? And if not now then when?
You can't afford to lose yourself again.

Our own movie.

Memories are just like scenes from a script.
Just like little movie clips,
And you really do deserve to look back on a beautiful movie,
Maybe not a great start, maybe not even a exciting middle,
maybe not even a really happy perfect end,
But we never know how long we will spend on this earth,
And people are never going to truly know are worth till we are gone,
Till your loved ones remember how you used to dance and sing
so out of tune to that certain song,
Till they realise you were the life jacket.
that stopped them from drowning and remembered
all the silly jokes you would say to them
when you noticed they were frowning,
One day we won't wake up and maybe you don't mind that right now.
because you are tired and have had enough,
But one day it will be over and maybe that brings you closure,
But while you are here, face that fear,
Be that kid do the things they did or didn't do and keep pushing through,
Life is never going to be easy and that's certainly true,
Act like your still young at heart, channel that hurt and create art,
don't care what people think
because things can change and happen as quick as we can blink,
There can be joy in the dark times,
Being happy isn't a crime, you're going to be fine,
Make those memories while you can
Live your life as if it's only just began,
If you love someone you tell them everyday you're able to,
And In the darkest of moments keep pushing through
Because after every uphill climb
or every mountain there's a beautiful view
And in the end all those memories will form a clip
which will form a movie,
And you Deserve a movie full of beauty
A life with no rules, a life that is free.

Depression is invisible.

Depression is so much more than laying in bed in the dark all day,
It's getting up and smiling even though you are not okay,
Depression is being the life of the party,
even when you feel empty inside,
So much so people don't know you lied in bed all night and cried
Depression is invisible,
Depression is giving motivational speeches to others
but when it comes to yourself you feel totally lost in the world
and want to hide under the covers,
Depression doesn't make you weak
or just a person with broken parts in fact people
with depression have the most kindest hearts,
They know what it's like to be in pain
and they know that pain is difficult to explain
and if your struggling they know you are not to blame,
they can empathise with you because they feel the exact same,
Depression is making jokes so others feel joy they are unable to
It's being the guide to help someone else push through
It's being the light for others
when you are in the dark it's thinking and feeling
If you were to disappear it wouldn't even leave a mark,
Depression doesn't have a look
and it certainly doesn't come with and manual or book
There is no guide everyday you just wake up
and say okay well at least I tried
Depression is invisible.

Tiny voice.

If there's Ever even a tiny voice that tells or wants you to carry on
and stay strong even though the louder voice is telling you it's wrong,
Then I want you to listen to that little voice,
listen to it and don't quit.
Because right now the thoughts that you're a burden,
your existence doesn't matter and that you are not enough,
Dealing with these everyday is really tough,
But just because you have a thought
it doesn't make it true,
don't let it take a hold of you,
because sometimes all it take is a little spark to get you out of the dark,
Sometimes fighting can make you feel like
your struggles were made up and that you are a liar,
Sometimes healing can feel like your jumping into a fire,
And it's scary so we can choose to jump into the fire
and risk getting burned
but even if we stay where we are we will still get hurt anyway
which I have recently learned,
It's a difficult choice
but my advice would be to listen to that little voice,
to not only survive but to fight to thrive,
and to engage in a battle of war
even when it doesn't seem worth fighting for.

When I fall into my depression.

When I fall into my depression I may not be myself
for awhile that smile may no longer be there
but that doesn't mean I no longer care,
Even if it seems we are drifting apart
even in the most darkest of times you are always in my heart,
I may not reply to your texts or calls,
I may break down or snap at you over something so small
I may push you away even when I want you to stay,
Or tell you I'm fine even when I'm not okay,
I may lash out and you may wonder what all that was about,
When I fall into my depression
I may cancel plans and stay in bed
No one would want you around my head said
So alone in the darkness I'll be instead,
When I fall into my depression
I may not be the same
but I'm sorry it's just the chemicals in my brain,
When I fall into my depression just know
I don't know when but you will see me again,
Sometime, someday
Right now the sun has gone
and I am in the grey, but I will be okay.

It's okay to be okay

I wanted to let you know it's okay to not be okay.
but I also wanted to say it's okay to be okay,
It's okay to not be suffering and/or in pain
and many people may feel confused by this but let me explain,
When we have spent so much of our life's unwell
it can almost become our identity
that people start to question whether people will still care
and love them if they were to get better mentally,
We can hold onto our illness as if that is all we are,
To afraid to let go which prevents us from moving on and going far
But to the person reading this I want you to know that if you let that go
you won't be on your own,
That you may have spent years of your life lost
but that does not mean you still can't find your way back home,
People will still care even if you're okay,
There love and care won't just go away,
So as difficult as things maybe,
being ill isn't your identity
and certainly isn't all other people see,
Years spent trapped, think about how great it would be to be free
But I just want to say,
It's okay to be okay
You don't need to compensate for it
You just need to live your life to the fullest and to never quit.

Social media.

Social media may portray we are okay ,
we seem so happy on our Instagram displays
We're fine,
I mean just take a look at our Facebook time-line.
Posting anything other then happiness and positivity would be a crime
So we compare why isn't my life like this?
Look at all the things people are up to and all that I've missed,
But the person who seems to have the best day of their life
may of had the worst day ever
but they put on a smile even though they're feeling under the weather,
On social media We may all look like we have it all together
but we never know what is going on for one another,
That's why it's important to be kind
because what you'll find
is that you never know what is going on in someone's mind
So yes social media maybe all smiles,
but they've maybe struggling for awhile,
You never know what's goes on behind closed doors
So take a pause,
Someone may not be as happy as they seem to be,
sometimes struggles you cannot see,
So be kind always.

The impact you make

Even when you are at your lowest because of you someone is at their highest,
Now this isn't a guilt trip I'm just saying you matter
and make a difference whether you believe it or not
even if you yourself are going through a lot,
You make people laugh and smile every single day
even when you are not okay,
You bring colour to the world even when you are in the grey,
If you were not here things really wouldn't be the same
and I know that may seem a selfish thing to say when you are in pain,
And question everyday if it matters if you were to go or stay,
But I promise you it would
and I would take all the hurt and upset away
from you if I could if you were to leave
Yes people would wake up and still breathe
but it would leave a hole inside like you wouldn't believe,
They'd want to tell you all the things they have achieved
and things you could have achieved too,
Knowing your missing out on things and your going to miss out on many more
because you didn't think there was anything left fighting for,
Your presence makes a difference on this earth,
I hope one day you are able to see your worth
To let go of the sadness and hurt
and everything you perceived as the norm and to battle through the storm,
And the love and care and kindness and compassion you have for everyone else.
I hope you afford to give some to yourself
because you deserve that,
you deserve that just like everyone else.
But what's important to remember is that just
because it's heavy right now doesn't mean it won't be lighter again
but when it's really heavy
we think how can this ever not be heavy again
but nothing lasts, there's a stronger version of you living in the future.
regardless of how heavy things get
It's okay if it's heavy and you don't know why don't drive yourself mad
trying to figure out why you feel how you feel,
Because there doesn't have to be an explanation and sometimes there isn't,
Other then the fact life is hard at times and can get heavy
which is when you need to take it easy,
One more time,
because one more time
will turn to one last time and things will be lighter.

One minute

One minute I'm ready to take on the world,
And then it feels like the world is going to end,
One minute I'm smiling
the next I'm too tired to play pretend,
I can feel everything and nothing all at the same time,
On the inside I'm hurting but on the outside 'I'm fine'
One minute I'm laughing the next I'm in pain but I keep it to myself
because this is all far too difficult to explain,
Because although people say it's just life it's very up and down
but how do I tell them the lows feel like I'm going to drown?
Because of your mind that's being cruel,
battling your mind everyday is the hardest battle of them all,
Because it can't be fixed by the things
you used to do when you were sad when you were small,
Because this is all so much more than just sadness
and at times life can feel like madness,
You feel like your too broken to mend
but apparently your not which is hard to comprehend,
Apparently you're not broken just a person with unmet needs
that doesn't define your value or dictate whether you will or will not succeed,
People tell me don't give up because it would be such a waste
What's hard to understand is
They say it wasn't your fault but it is your responsibility
to heal and deal with the pain and the trauma
that I never even asked for in the first place.

We all have a story

I was walking round the park today,
Everything was a bit grey,
While I was walking round this park
I realised that no one can hear me or see me,
That They don't know I'm in the dark,
Which made me think we really never know
what someone else is going through
None of us have a clue,
Someone may have just lost their brother or their mother,
We never know what's going on for one another,
Maybe that person is unwell but your unable to tell because they look fine
But they're having an internal battle all the time,
Maybe someone is in a relationship they don't want to be in
or maybe someone has no money or home and they get there dinner out of a bin,
So maybe it is a very simple thing as to just be kind
as we really have no idea what's going on in someone's mind,
A simple smile or compassion or kindness
they may not have received for awhile,
That they may feel seen that the past
doesn't and hasn't defined them no matter
All the dark places they've been,
So maybe we need to treat everyone
as if we don't know what they've been through
or going through,
Because I know for me I've battled things no one even knew,
We will never truly know what someone is going through
till we have walked in their shoes,
So this is your reminder to be kinder
And if your the one walking round in the park while you are in the dark
You are loved.

To those who want the pain to end

If your struggling with suicidal thoughts/ idealisation/
feelings then this is for you,
As I know how difficult they are to push through,
Now I'm not going to say it will all be okay
because right now it doesn't feel that way
and it all being better I can't guarantee
But you can listen to me,
Because I know what it's like to want to be free
I want you to know that it's okay,
it's okay to delay the decision and put it off for another day,
And you can do that over and over again,
Look I know you're in so much pain
And everyday is just the same,
Trying to hold on when all you want to do is let go,
believe me I know, okay I know,
I know what it's like to have no hope
when you feel like things are too difficult to cope.
Where there doesn't feel like there is no way out
and that's scary there is no doubt,
But maybe in time you'll find this is just an illness in your mind
and that depression isn't at all that kind,
Maybe someone may smile at you on the street,
you never know who you will meet,
Maybe you'll fall in love,
And you won't get to experience that if you were to fly up above,
And I know right now none of that matters to you
Because you don't think your able to get through
But maybe there will be a day,
a day that's not so grey,
And maybe as hard as it is and will be to fight,
You'll eventually see some kind of light,
That people are there, that people do care and you are enough
But right now things are a little tough,
But that doesn't mean things always will be,
And if they ever do
I feel like you deserve the chance to see,
Life without the misery,
It's not weak to speak
It's important as things kept inside can become heavy,
So don't quit
And as someone once told me
You never know life may get better. Make sure you're there to see it.

A suffocating loop.

With depression your days turn into one suffocating loop
With the days never ending
Your sick of pretending
Sick of saying 'oh no I'm fine'
When you're battling your mind all the time.
It's a battle to breathe but this pain, this suffering no one believes.
Because you're the happy one right?
No one knows you have to wake up everyday and fight.
Struggling to see the end of the tunnel where there's supposedly light.
No one believes because you wake up with a smile,
But you've been in pain for awhile,
Where you no longer live but exist,
There will be no enjoyment on your to do list
Because every task becomes a chore,
But you don't want to come across as a bore
So you pretend to be okay
and everyone tells you life's too short
to be anything other than happy,
But do they really think I choose to be this way?
Maybe to a certain degree I do
but that's only because sadness is what I'm used to,
and you get to the stage you feel like
Being sad is just you,
Stuck in the never ending loop,
your mind is a war zone
Without any troops
Sometimes we indulge in the sadness
it's all we know and it can be hard to let go.
Depression is a suffocating loop, you lose the concept of time,
How are you? It's oh I'm fine.
Depression will drag you down till it feels like you'll drown
and can no longer turn things around,
But don't let the darkness consume you,
because although right now it's just always these suffocating loops,
But eventually in time you'll find your troops.

<u>Healing.</u>
Healing is messy and confusing,
so much so it can be hard to know if your doing it right
Because of that you think it is worth the fight?
But On the other side of pain
it still could be a little messy but maybe a little less rain.
May not be all sunshine and rainbows
but there may be a little more highs and not only lows.
Healing can still mean tears I mean so right so
You're trying to heal from trauma or pain
you've experienced throughout the years.
But maybe on the other side of pain
is peace or little moments of peace at least.
And maybe during healing it all just isn't suddenly okay.
But maybe you'll wake up and it won't be as grey.
You're not numbing yourself
from the things that have happened anymore.
And even though feeling it hurts to the core.
You're doing it.
Even though the things that may have happened
in your life weren't planned.
They shouldn't of happened
so no wonder why it's difficult to understand
But you're doing it.
Healing is a difficult process
and it doesn't mean your invalid or you suffered less
You've suffered enough, kept on going when things have been so tough.
Healing is messy and confusing
doesn't mean what you experienced didn't happen,
it just means a different life you are choosing.
And that's a brave thing to do.
Healing is possible. I believe in you.
Healing from trauma doesn't automatically mean everything is okay.
Healing can still mean having a bad day,
It can be sadness causing emotions you never even felt before,
Maybe it could even be feeling the emotions even more.
And you're wondering why am I still feeling this way when I'm healing?
You're no longer using self harm
,restriction of food, whatever you did to feel numb.
You're letting the emotions naturally come.
And as uncomfortable as it maybe,
It's an important process to be free.
If your trying to heal and you still feeling depressed
it's all part of healing because all the feelings you suppressed ,
so don't just quit.
Don't just say' well this is it'
It's a process, and eventually the pain and struggle

will become less and less
You're doing your best.
This is going to sound weird
but feeling these things while healing could mean your doing something right.
So remember that whenever you want to give up the fight

Warning signs

Behind every I don't care is emotion,
behind every I don't know is knowledge,
behind every 'I'm fine.'
Is a person who isn't fine.
Which is something that I say all the time.
I have lost friends to suicide,
That morning I heard her laughing, that night I got told she had died.
We listen to someone and believe there 'I'm fine.
Little did we know it could be a warning sign.
It could look like giving out the things they own.
It could be isolating alone in their home.
It could be pushing loved ones away,
'How are you?' 'I'm okay' they always say.
They don't want to be a burden,
they don't want to be a pain,
so they keep all the hurt they feel inside even if it drives them insane.
It could be covered up by a laugh,
It could be covered up by a smile
They could look okay but they could be suffering for a while.
So check in with those you're close to.
You never know things they're trying to get through,
Or things they are trying to overcome,
try and be there because everyone needs someone.
Or at least be kind, you never know what is going on in someone's mind.

Don't make that decision.

If your on the edge with your goodbye letters on the ledge,
Feeling like the world wants you gone,
feeling like you no longer can be strong.
Well you're wrong and you do belong.
Scared and unsure to what the future will bring
I know your holding on by a piece of string
But what if you were to just about to let go
And you get a text message from someone you know,
They let you know you're not alone
and that they know you're facing battles
that you don't have to deal with on your own.
Or you look out the window feeling so low,
but your favourite song starts playing on the radio.
You remember an old memory,
like having to stand up in assembly,
Or an object in your room that meant a lot to you remembering that,
that got you through nights you didn't think you could do.
You pour the medication down in the kitchen sink
and you have a little think.
You don't feel it but you are loved
and it would destroy your family and friends
if you were to fly up above.
I know it may seem easier to end it today
but maybe one day things will be okay,
You've experienced the worst,
you're yet to experience the best.
Life will constantly put you to the test.
Don't base a decision like that on a bad day month or year,
it's okay to fear there are people that are here to catch your tears.
There's more happiness to come,
so please don't be done,
one day you'll be able to look back and be able to say
'I have won'

Here for the bad not only the good.

We tend to ignore how we feel inside
Ignore the fact that we've cried.
Ignore the pain, we just label it as just being sad
although it's a chemical imbalance in our Brain.
We don't tend to talk about the bad only the good
I think that's why mental health is so misunderstood.
Social media is filled with happy times.
But if you met up with a friend
would talking about how you really felt be such a crime,
instead of just saying your fine,
We tend to compare but perhaps
if we talk about the deep but real things
people will be more inclined to share.
Because the truth is the 'happy one' the one that's got it all together.
Are doing their best to keep it together.
While realistically feeling under the weather.
The one who's the class clown is actually feeling down.
Yeah talking about how we feel it is sad
but it's real, it's how you feel and surely
I can speak on behalf of everyone on this
that I'd rather hear about your pain, your sadness then your eulogy.
Life stops for no one, everyone facing battles there trying to overcome.
Maybe we should share a bit more to show the younger generations
that the negative emotions are okay to explore.
That they don't have to go through it alone anymore.
That it's okay to share and there will always be someone listening and there.
That someone does actually care about the bad and not only the good.
Now, that is what needs to be more understood.

You're in there somewhere.

Even in the times we are most in the dark,
where we feel as if we have lost all our spark.
People around can still see the light
, wanting us to grab that part no matter how small and fight.
They know we are still in there, somewhere.
So they cherish the day they see you but no matter what they're there.
The good, the bad and the ugly.
Catching our tears, working through fears
and lending their listening ears.
They don't see you as the sad one,
just having battles you're trying to overcome.
They still see you through the pain.
Behind that, behind all that is you.
Not too broken, not worthless, but you
Every now and then the you comes out
and they see you and think this is what you're about.
The smile they see every once in a while.
They want to see you win.
Mental illness can be a devastating thing.
But somewhere you're there.
And people do care.
It can be hard to accept or even to allow.
But you don't have to deal with it alone now.
Every version of you exists still,
the broken you crying on the floor exists in your mind.
But In your friend's mind you're the girl that's kind.
So meaningful and pure,
So funny and makes people laugh deep to the core.
But you say 'that's not you anymore'
You're too far gone you think. Well you're wrong.
You're in there somewhere.
Right now you're just filled with despair.
But people around can still see the light
and they want you to grab that part no matter how small and fight.

<u>Your story isn't over.</u>

Your story isn't over.
It feels like it is but I promise you it isn't.
I know everyday your mind is like living in a prison.
Feeling like a mission to get through.
But your story isn't over, and that couldn't be anymore true.
If only you knew. If only I knew.
Because this isn't written by a random person
but a person who's been there
and your pain I don't want it to worsen.
This is written from the heart
but also insight from my mind,
As I know from time to time our minds aren't very kind.
Questioning our reality maybe this is just our mentality.
Thinking this is all we will be,
just sad and wanting to be free, desperately.
But no matter the pain inside.
No matter how many tears you have cried.
Your story isn't over.
And I hope one day you'll see that right now
is not all what your life will be.
Your story isn't over
and one day you will find your closure.

You're not what you have been through

Your trauma and people around you have made you believe
you are a terrible person,
That just by your existence peoples life you worsen,
But let me tell you that's simply not true,
Because despite everything you've been through,
Despite all the times being hurt you never let your heart turn to stone,
And I'm so sorry for all the battles you have had to get through alone
But the you that you have become
is someone you'd feel safe with when you were young,
You always check in with others to make sure they are okay
As you know what it's like to feel pain
and hurt and you don't want anyone else to feel that way,
Your smile just brightens up the day,
Your kindness your humour you're personality
People's opinions don't define your reality,
You never deserved to go through the things you did
You were only a kid,
You didn't deserve any of it at all
But once you make it to the other side,
You become a much more loving and understanding individual,
I hope one day you will see yourself in a different light
because honestly you make the dark areas in life much more bright,
You bring so much good simply by just being a around,
While you yourself are lost you still help others to be found
Despite what you may believe,
Or the love and care as a kid you may of not received,
You deserve so much good and more,
And one day you will create a life that's worth fighting for.

Setting yourself free.

Once you learn how to set yourself free,
From all of the pain and all of the misery,
You will soon start to see how wonderful life can really be,
That it's okay and you not failing if in life
you don't know what you're going to do,
It's an achievement just getting through,
Not knowing what you want from life
can be a scary but also beautiful thing to,
Maybe some things you will hate but you just try something new,
Because no matter how bad things get
you will always have the opportunity to start a clean slate,
And it may be hell to begin with
but then it may soon start to become great,
And you may have set backs and that's alright
It just makes us appreciate it more when things start to feel more bright,
And you may feel lost right now
Happiness feels hard to allow
You may not feel like you deserve the chance to live
But let me tell you this you have so much to give
A purpose in life doesn't have to be anything big,
That isn't what a purpose is,
As we grow we to start to know
that we have to let go in order to move on,
And sometimes being strong can feel wrong,
And we feel empty and like we don't belong
But there will be a time
One day down the line,
Where life doesn't feel so heavy
And grey where things are finally starting to feel okay
Where it doesn't feel hard to breathe
Where you don't even think about if you should stay or leave
You start living a life that past you never believed could be achieved
You will see that life really is about the little things
And you will see all of the wonderful, messy,
terrifying beautiful moments life will bring
And sometimes life stings
But I hope you stick around long enough to see
How once you set yourself free
How wonderful life can be,
It can happen to you even a person
who doesn't think they will make it through,
Because you can find peace while living
This isn't the end for you it's the beginning

<u>I lay there</u>

I lay there.
While the world is still spinning around,
Throughout all the seasons
the sunshine in the sky,
To the snow falling and hitting the ground,
While the world Carries on
I lay there still
Not hurting or in pain
As I'm too tired to feel,
As it turns from night to day
And all I've done has been in bed turning the opposite way,
I just wait for it to all be okay
My body to heavy and achy to climb out of bed,
Bad thoughts and anxiety making a home in my head
Everything seems to go so fast,
I know that nothing lasts
But what I also know
Is in my world time goes slow,
Weeks, months, years go by
Time just flashes before my eyes
Yet i lay here still,
Too tired to feel
This isn't no way to live I know that's true
But I don't know any other way to get through
But anyway it's too late to change
And anyway feeling anything other then the way I feel would feel strange,
So here I lay,
While it's sunny outside but in my mind it's grey
While the birds chirp and kids laugh while they play,
I lay there and say
I hope I'll be able to feel that one day.

Unconditional love

Because all I want is for someone to be there.
Someone to listen,
someone to care,
For someone to listen about my day
And listen without judgement to the things I have to say,
To hold me tight and tell me it's all going to be alright,
even if it doesn't feel that way,
To love and be loved in return
For love that I don't have to earn,
Love that is unconditional,
Sometimes I wish I was still a kid,
I wish that I was small,
So they can wrap me up in there arms
And block out all of the things that may cause me harm,
They will be my human shield,
But now I'm on this battlefield,
All on my own,
Trying to find my way back home,
Because I say I don't need anyone
But I do,
I tell you I'm fine on my own but that isn't quite true,
We all need love and care,
As much as I don't want to admit I want it,
I need it and it's a common thing
As humans we all share,
So as vulnerable as it feels to say
I wish I had someone to tell me it's going to be okay
Even if it doesn't feel that way,
That someone who even when I'm stumbling around in the dark for awhile,
Although my world is covered in darkness,
They still manage to make me smile.
To love me throughout the good the bad and the ugly
To love and care about me throughout it all
To receive love and care that is unconditional.

Maybe I am an attention seeker

For many years I've been labelled like most people
who suffer with mental Illness,
as attention seeker,
Which I took as a negative and an insult,
Which made me feel like my struggles were invalidated,
Which impacted me asking for help as a result,
But maybe they're right in what they say
But maybe we just need to look at it in another way,
For Some of us,
Proper care and love wasn't received,
Being unwell or suffering we unintentionally got our needs met,
And it became a way of love and care finally being achieved,
Care, love, affection and attention
is such an important factor for a developing brain,
Without those things,
We have had to learn how to survive just about to deal with the pain,
To be loved and cared for we all crave,
Asking for help requires being brave,
We all attention seek,
Some may feel as if they don't get the right help
or people don't listen when they speak,
As a baby we cry and it takes people time to figure out why,
Because we know they need some kind of help in a certain way,
Our initial thought isn't them attention seeking it's making sure they are okay,
They maybe hungry or be in pain,
It's a form for asking for help as they can't do it on their own
and as we grow older we do the same
So if you ever get called an attention seeker
That's okay,
We just need to start to look at it in a different way.

Stay.

You're not a lost cause,
Your just lost,
Your life is too precious to give up,
You are to precious although it may not feel that way
And you don't believe things will ever be okay
But don't make a permanent decision
Based on a temporary feeling
Even if giving up and not having to think sounds appealing
But one day you will laugh like you never have before,
And you won't feel like the way you used to or do right now anymore,
There will be days where it may get bad,
But you got through it back then you can make it through again
I know you're tired and you just want it all to end,
I know you put on a smile and play pretend
That your fine all of the time
It's going to all be over one day
So just stay,
Just a little bit longer,
The thoughts maybe loud and unbearable and heavy,
But you can be stronger
But most importantly you are not alone
And you don't have to face these battles and demons all on your own
You may feel like you have no one right now
But there's people who love you and will be there if you allow
Your not a burden or a pain
You may yet to meet a loving understanding person
who's experienced the same
Your loved beyond Measure and there is no pressure to be okay
People love you for you and we wouldn't want you any other way
We just hope and pray you choose to stay
But not only because it'll hurt and we will miss you
But because you have a life to live
And despite what has happened or what you have been through
You can still create a life with meaning
And it's so true
Just your existence makes an impact
Your smile brightens someone's day
People love you
And I hope you choose to stay,

Messages of hope

Written by family and friends…

Including favourite quotes/poems
and handwritten messages
To give you hope

"There are lots of things I can't promise you,
can't promise you sunshine and rainbows
everyday and I can't promise you every dream
you've ever dreamt. However I can promise.
that there will be days that don't feel quite as
difficult as others, I promise that you will find a
purpose other than being ill and I promise that
you will not regret choosing to live. Recovery
can be a lifelong battle but I promise you, you
are strong enough to fight it. There is a life out
there waiting for you to live it. There is a life out
there without the pain and suffering you
currently have to endure. There is a happy life
out there that you deserve to live. It is okay to
end a chapter of suffering and begin a new
chapter of happiness and hope."

"I never used to believe
this, so it's okay if right
Now you don't either. But
things do change.. with
time and resilience the
world really can get
brighter. The unbearable,
can become surprisingly
bearable. Just keep
going."

"You've come such a long way,
and dealt with many difficult days. Because of this,
I know you will continue to make progress

and, you will be better able
to deal with difficult times in the future
I don't think you yet realise how strong your inner self is.
Believe me, you will.
That will be the tool for a much much brighter future."

"Part of a favourite poem written by -Rupi Kaur

Grow our own
flowers. The universe delivered us with the
light and the seeds. We might not hear it at
times but the music is always on it just needs
to be turned up louder. So for as long as there
is breath in our lungs we must keep dancing.
-Rupi Kaur

'I love the saying every time we are present
there is a little more light in the world for everyone.'

"Strength doesn't come from what you can do it comes from overcoming,
the things you once thought you couldn't do."

"One day or day one,
time to motivate and make goals happen
You decide"

"Recovery is remembering who you are and using your strengths
To become all that you were meant to be."

'Never look down at your feet, only at the stars!'

"You will have good days and bad days;
sometimes it might even feel like the world is caving in on you
. Life can be tough sometimes.
But the key word in that last sentence is sometimes.
You will cry tears of sadness but also tears of laughter.
You will have losses and gains. Life, however, is truly beautiful.
Those crisp mornings with clear blue skies; throwing snowballs at your
friends;
watching sunsets on the beach with a BBQ and so so much more
. Each day is a new opportunity to progress and grow.
Life is a journey; it will have its ups and downs.
You belong in this world. You deserve to thrive and feel true happiness,
no matter who you are or what has happened in your past.
If you're reading this, you have survived every single one of your bad days.
All of them. Those days that were harrowing- you survived them.
You are strong for that. So stay
Stay a little longer and discover how wonderful this world can be."

Having lived with mental health problems for many years, the advise I would give to other people in a similar situation is to never give up - I was once in that place where I thought recovery was never going to be possible and I would never have a life worth living, but actually, if you yourself really want to get better and recover then it is possible. Only you can decide that. No one else can do it for you.

"Your wound is probably not your fault, but your healing is your responsibility"

'for everyone in pain, please know, that this too shall pass...'

Printed in Great Britain
by Amazon

32284472R00050